This planner belongs to

Your

photo

here

How to use your planner

Monday	Tuesday	Wednesday	Thursday
8	9	fill the dates in these boxes	
		17 Field trip to ☺ Aquarium	
	Write your plan for the day		

Note to self

Draw a theme for this month

draw anything

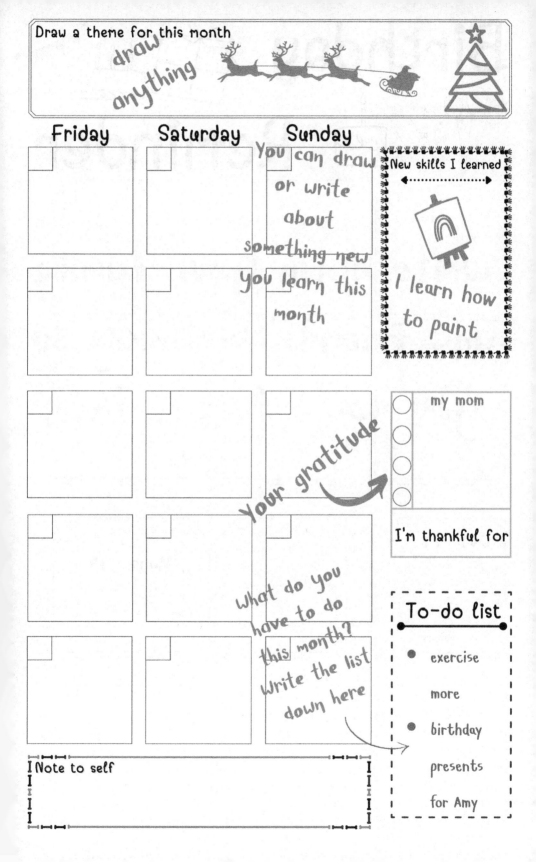

Friday	Saturday	Sunday
		You can draw or write about something new you learn this month

New skills I learned

I learn how to paint

my mom

I'm thankful for

Your gratitude

What do you have to do this month? Write the list down here

To-do list

- exercise more
- birthday presents for Amy

Note to self

Birthday Reminder

JAN | FEB | MAR

Write down your family
and friends' birthday so
you don't forget them

APR | MAY | JUN

JUL
Carl - 24

AUG

SEP
Mona - 19

OCT | NOV | DEC

you can color them!

Let's do this

My Schedule

Semester:

Period	Monday	Tuesday	Wednesday	Thursday	Friday

Semester:

Period	Monday	Tuesday	Wednesday	Thursday	Friday

My Schedule

Semester:

Period	Monday	Tuesday	Wednesday	Thursday	Friday

Semester:

Period	Monday	Tuesday	Wednesday	Thursday	Friday

My Reading Log

Book Name	Author	Start	Finish

Birthday Reminder

JAN

FEB

MAR

APR

MAY

JUN

JUL

AUG

SEP

OCT

NOV

DEC

Monday	Tuesday	Wednesday	Thursday

Note to self

Draw a theme for this month

Friday	Saturday	Sunday

New skills I learned

I'm thankful for

To-do list

Note to self

Monday	Tuesday	Wednesday	Thursday

Note to self

Draw a theme for this month

Friday

Saturday

Sunday

New skills I learned
←·····················→

I'm thankful for

To-do list

Note to self

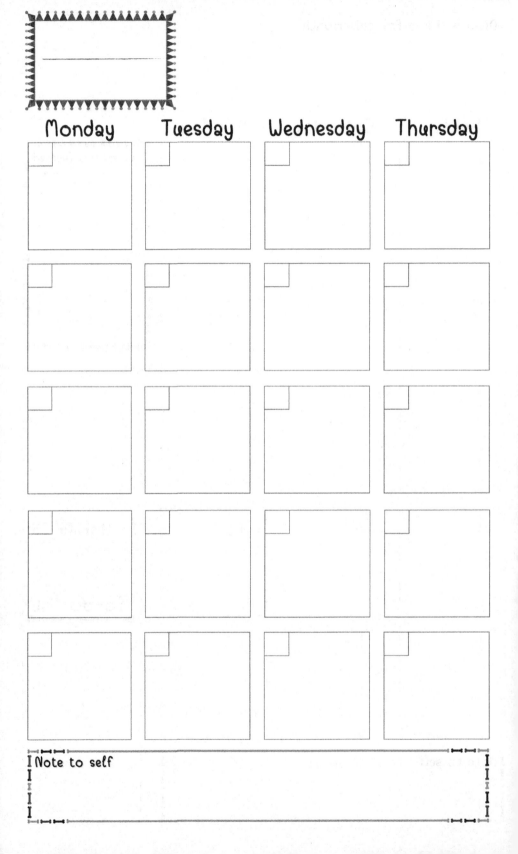

Monday	Tuesday	Wednesday	Thursday

Note to self

Draw a theme for this month

Friday

Saturday

Sunday

New skills I learned

I'm thankful for

To-do list

Note to self

Monday

Tuesday

Wednesday

Thursday

Note to self

Draw a theme for this month

Friday   ## Saturday   ## Sunday

New skills I learned

I'm thankful for

To-do list

Note to self

Monday	Tuesday	Wednesday	Thursday

Note to self

Draw a theme for this month

Friday

Saturday

Sunday

New skills I learned

I'm thankful for

To-do list

Note to self

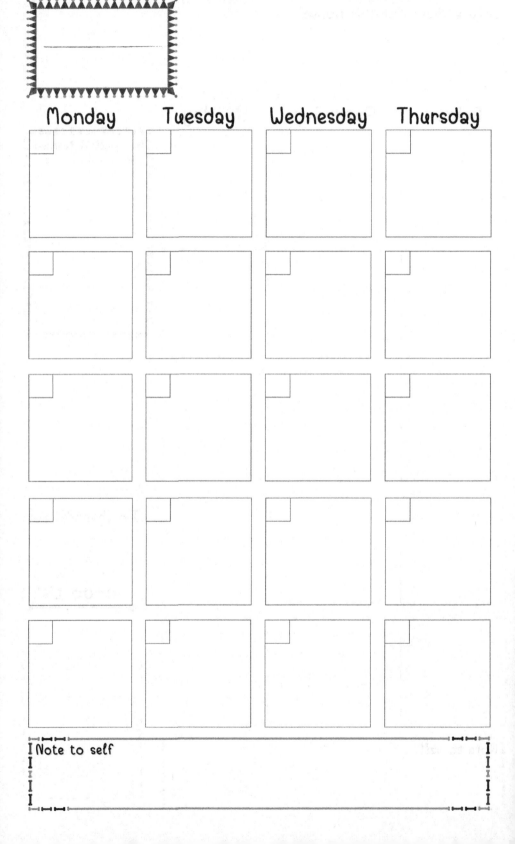

Monday   Tuesday   Wednesday   Thursday

Note to self

Draw a theme for this month

Friday

Saturday

Sunday

New skills I learned

I'm thankful for

To-do list

Note to self

Monday Tuesday Wednesday Thursday

Note to self

Draw a theme for this month

Friday   Saturday   Sunday

New skills I learned

I'm thankful for

To-do list

Note to self

Monday	Tuesday	Wednesday	Thursday

Note to self

Draw a theme for this month

Friday

Saturday

Sunday

New skills I learned

I'm thankful for

To-do list

Note to self

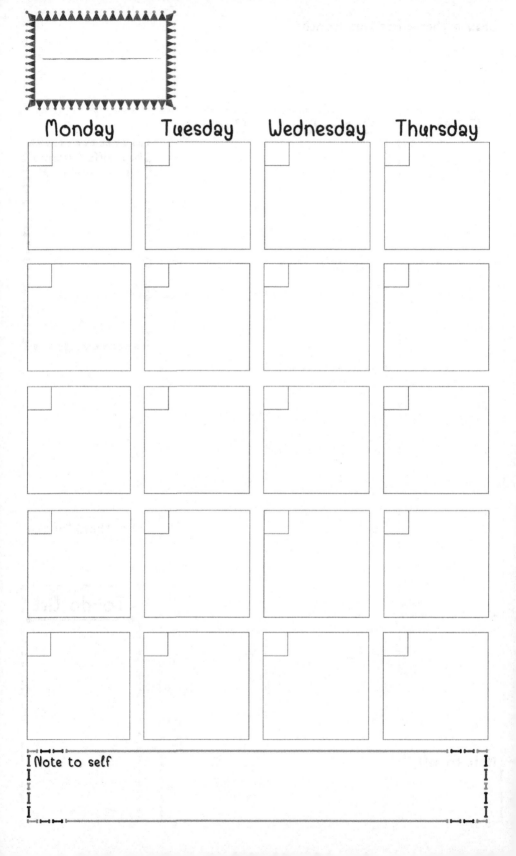

Monday Tuesday Wednesday Thursday

Note to self

Draw a theme for this month

Friday
Saturday
Sunday

New skills I learned

I'm thankful for

To-do list

Note to self

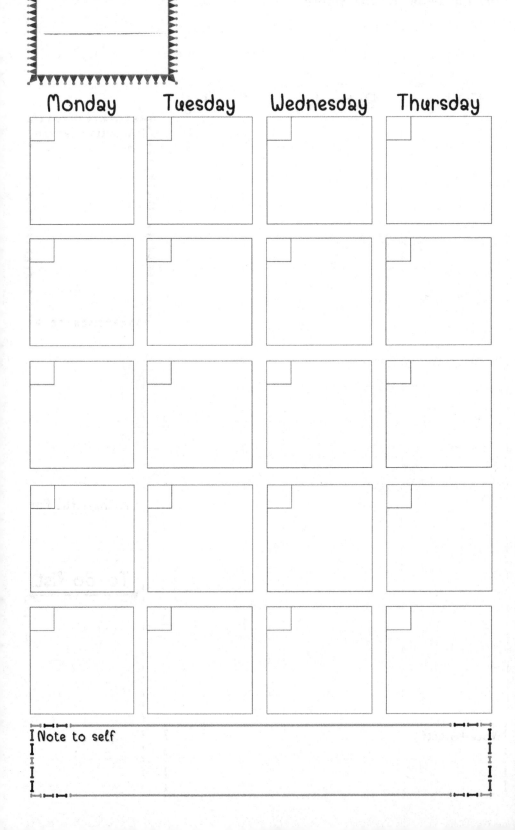

Monday

Tuesday

Wednesday

Thursday

Note to self

Draw a theme for this month

Friday

Saturday

Sunday

New skills I learned

I'm thankful for

To-do list

Note to self

Monday	Tuesday	Wednesday	Thursday

Note to self

Draw a theme for this month

Friday   Saturday   Sunday

New skills I learned

I'm thankful for

To-do list

Note to self

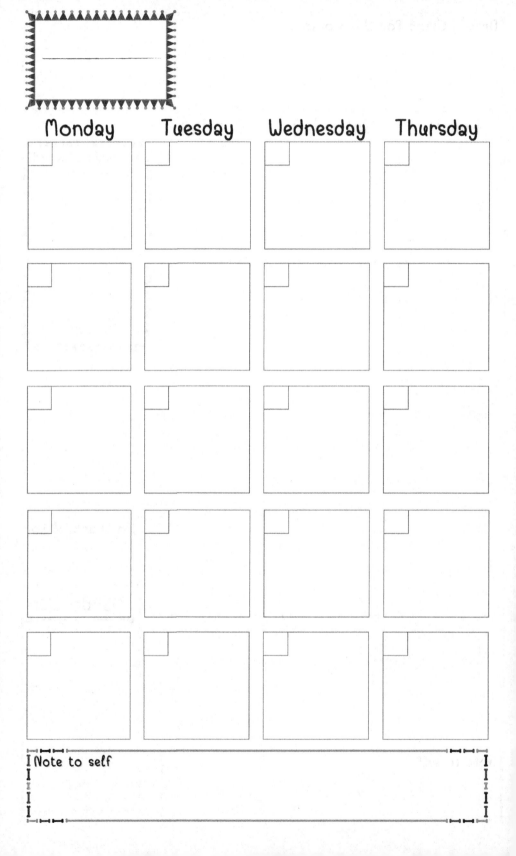

Monday

Tuesday

Wednesday

Thursday

Note to self

Draw a theme for this month

Friday	Saturday	Sunday

New skills I learned

I'm thankful for

To-do list

Note to self

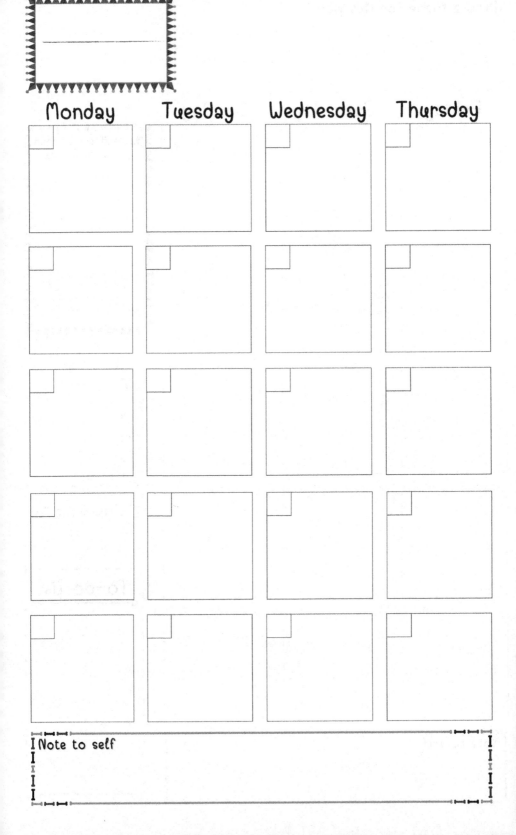

Monday | Tuesday | Wednesday | Thursday

Note to self

Draw a theme for this month

Friday

Saturday

Sunday

New skills I learned

I'm thankful for

To-do list

Note to self

Monday	Tuesday	Wednesday	Thursday

Note to self

Draw a theme for this month

Friday	Saturday	Sunday

New skills I learned

◀ • • • • • • • • • • • ▶

I'm thankful for

To-do list

Note to self

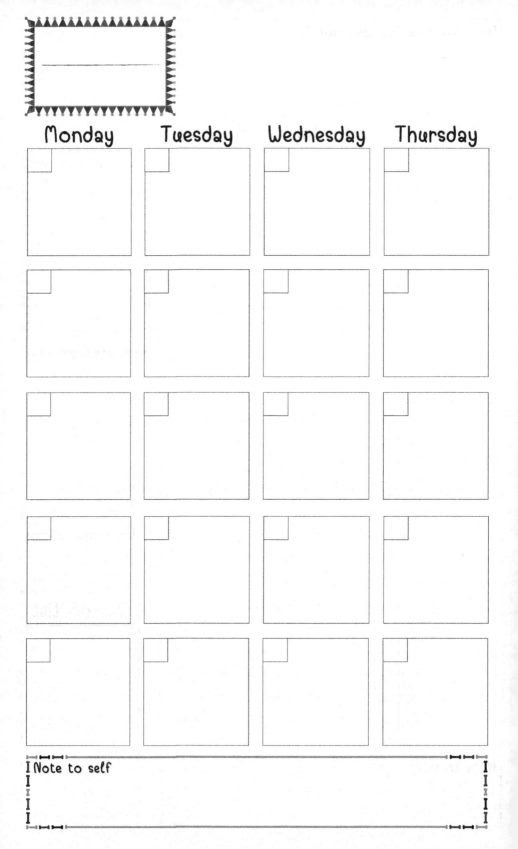

Monday	Tuesday	Wednesday	Thursday

Note to self

Draw a theme for this month

Friday   ## Saturday   ## Sunday

New skills I learned

I'm thankful for

To-do list

Note to self

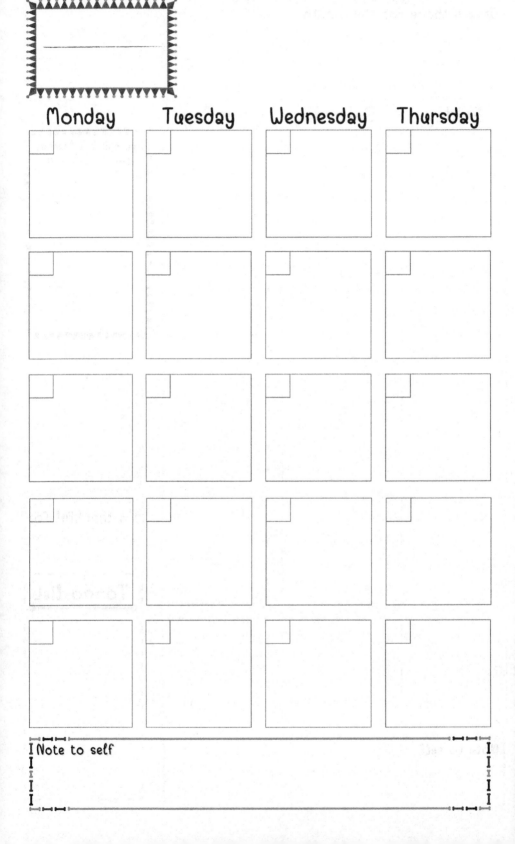

Monday	Tuesday	Wednesday	Thursday

Note to self

Draw a theme for this month

Friday

Saturday

Sunday

New skills I learned

I'm thankful for

Note to self

To-do list

A a B b C c D d

E e F f G g H h

I i J j K k L l

M m N n O o

P p Q q R r S s

T t U u V v

W w X x Y y Z z

apple

basketball

candles

desk

elephant

fish

ghost

hat

ice-cream

jellyfish

kite

ladder

monkey

nest

ocean

pig

queen

rabbit

scorpion

turtle

umbrella

vegetables

whale

xylophone

yo-yo

zebra

Let's see how many words can you fill in these pages

you can write

anywhere you like

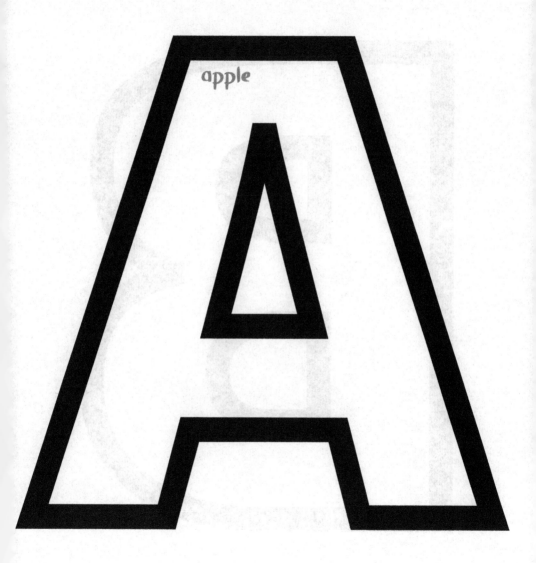

baseball

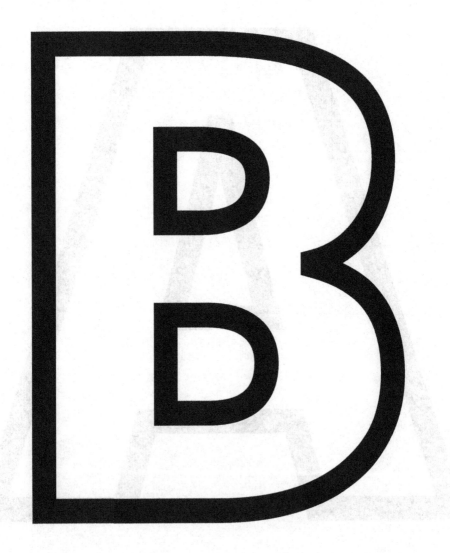

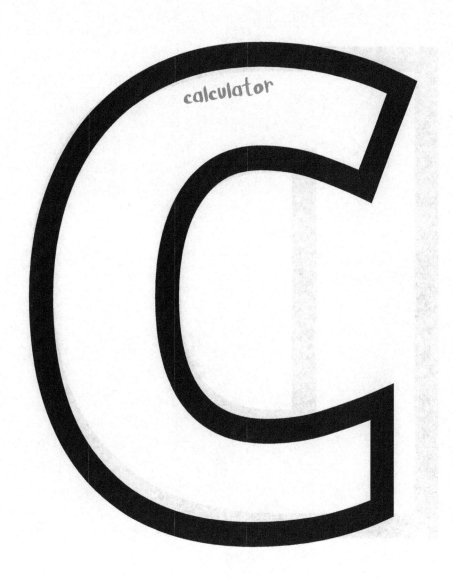
calculator

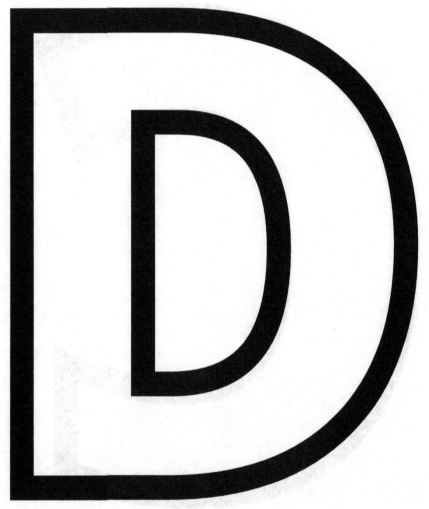

dog

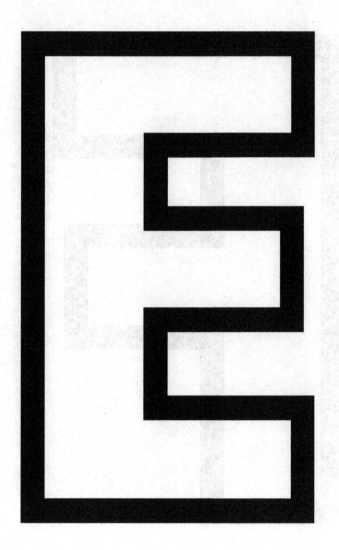

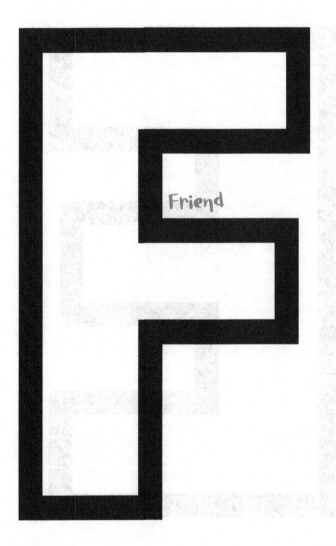
Friend

G

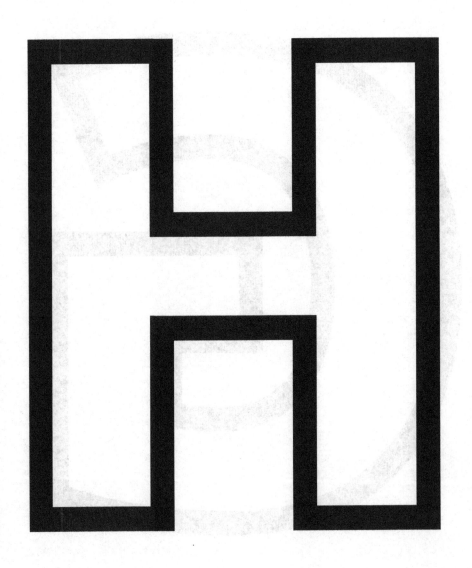

K

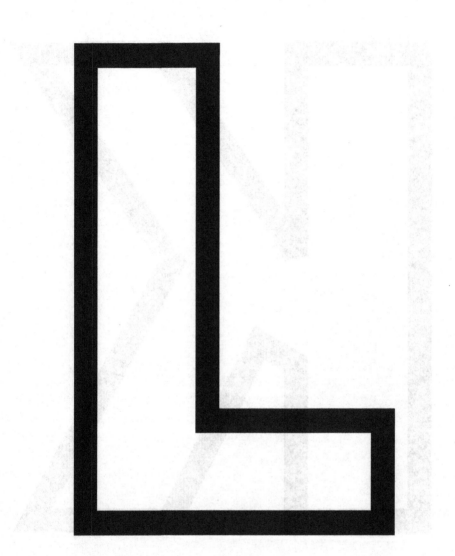

M

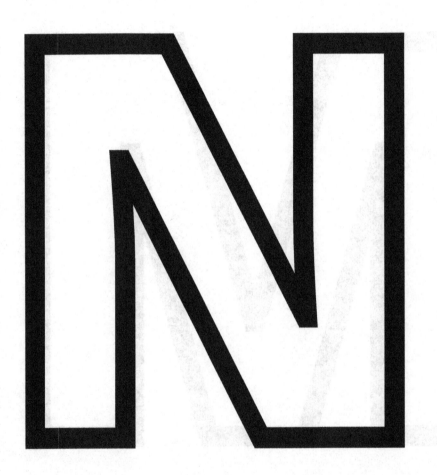

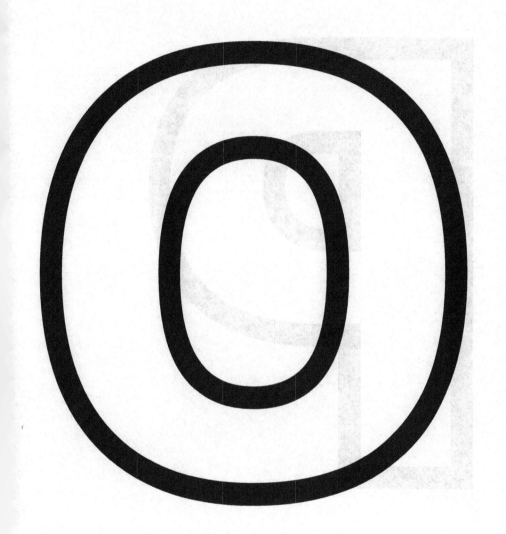

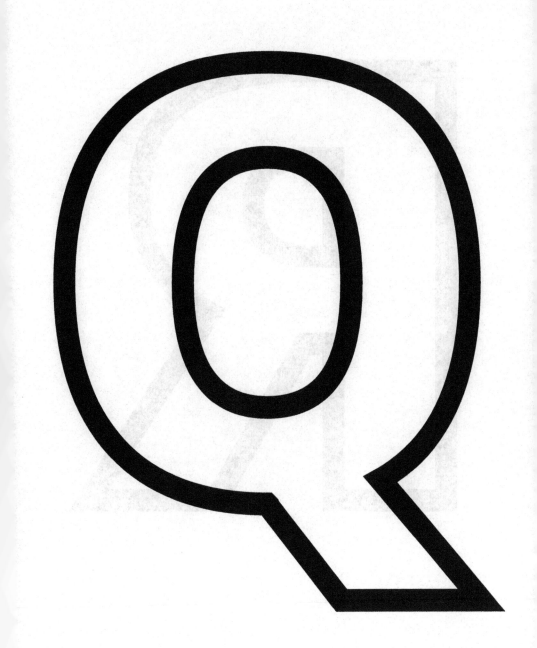

R

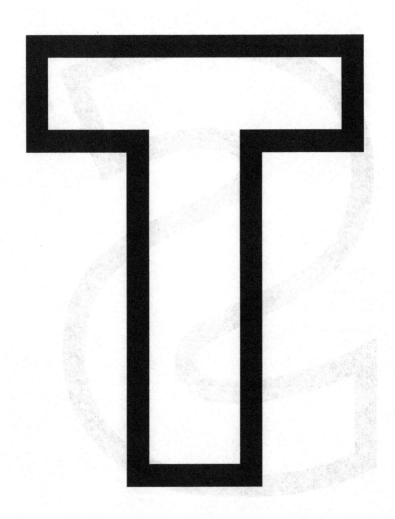

X

Z

Flags of the World

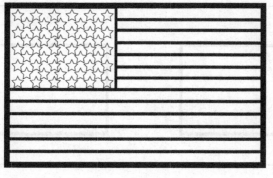

what's this flag?

_____

How many flags do you know?

Let's draw and color them!

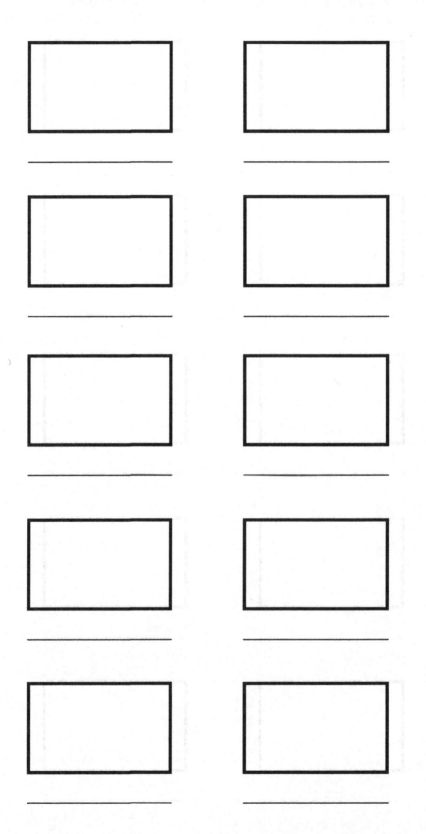

Let's boost

your

creativity

Draw yourself

Draw your favorite food

Draw your favorite fruits & vegetables

Draw your best friend

Draw your favorite animals

Fill this house with doors, windows, and whatever you like

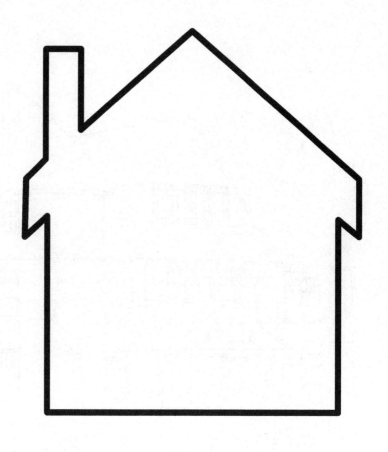

Color this house and fill the sky

Fill the ocean

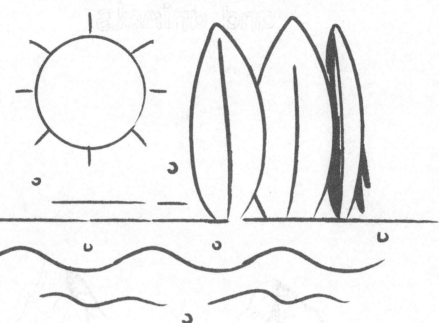

Let's add more trees and animals

Let's add 8 hands for the octopus

Let's draw an animal

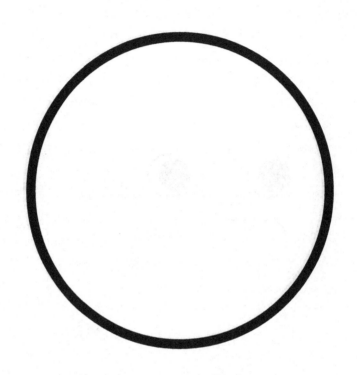

Memory Snap

Draw your day or put a

photo you took here.

Then you can write about

your special day

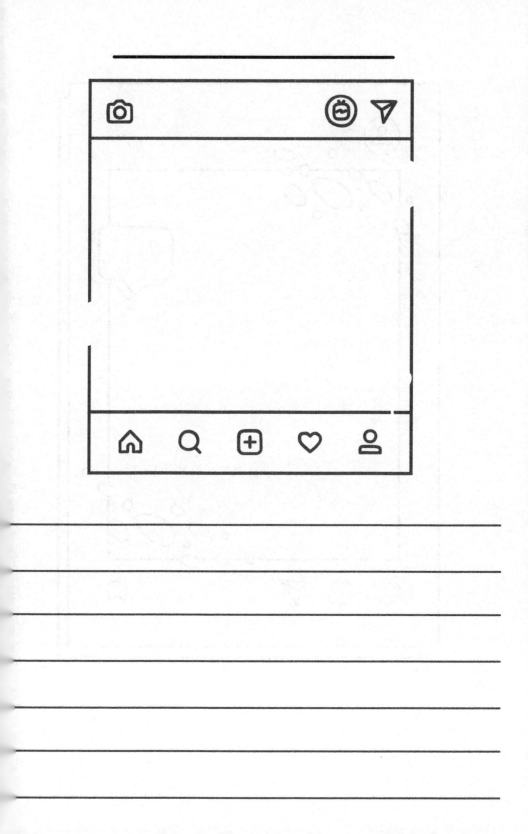

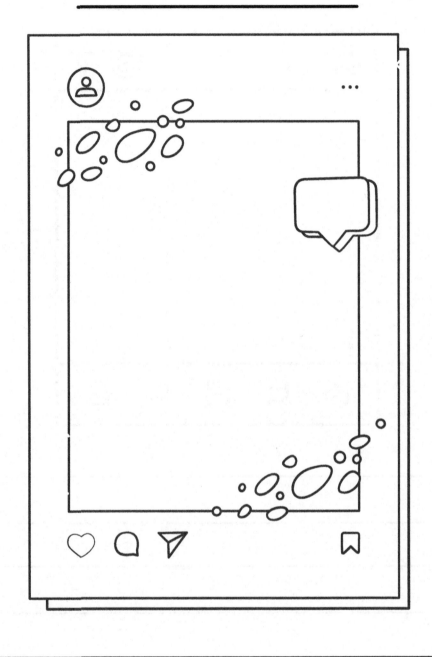

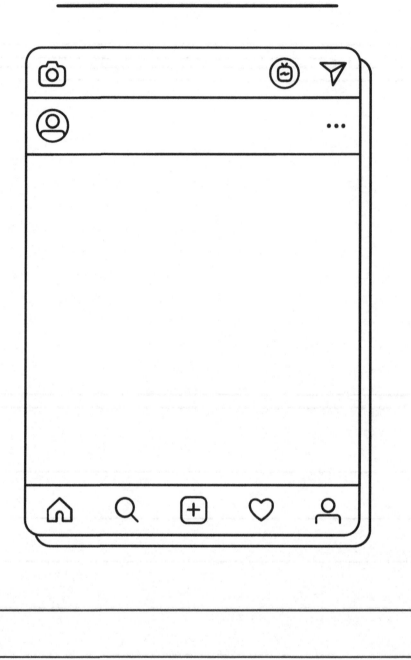

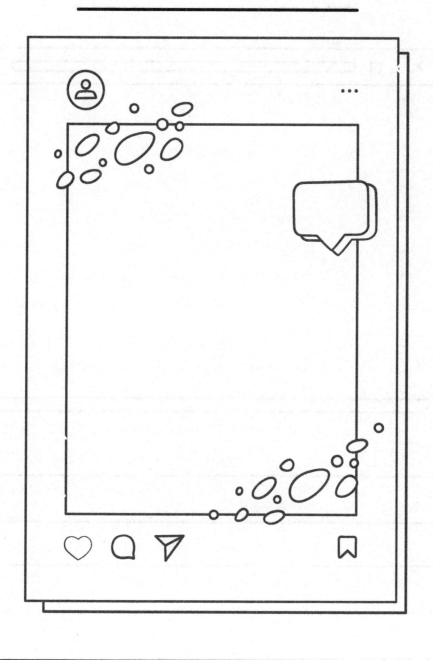

My Notes

My Notes

My Notes

My Notes

My Notes

My Notes

My Notes

My Notes

Made in the USA
Coppell, TX
14 November 2024

40262931R00066